MR LIZARD

Paul Parry

Cover design by Jonathan Cooksley

Edited by Susan Bush

Typesetting by Charlotte Mouncey

First edition published in 2017 by pmsl publishing (Parry Media Services Limited)

ISBN 978-0-9572531-4-8

www.PaulParry.com/MrLizard

For Shiana, Mischa, Harry and Phoebe,
and young people everywhere.

CONTENTS

ACKNOWLEDGEMENTS

Enormous gratitude, as always, to my family: Sholée, Shiana, Mischa, my mum, my dad, Dan, Saira, Yasmin, Arin, Hannah, Di, James, Showky and Patti.

Special thanks to Susan Bush for her brilliant editing and improving my work hugely.

And more than just a hat tip to these other great people:

Big Alan, Big Al, Big Jon, James Altucher, Corbett Barr, Sam Biggerstaff, Lionel Birnie, Alain de Botton, Peter Bowerman, Sir Dave Brailsford, Bob Burg, Warren Cass, Jarvis Cocker, Stuart Conroy, Larry David, Carol Dweck, Ben Edwards, Matt Edwards, Pierre Franckh, Lady Gaga, Stuart Gill, Graaarm, Nick Green, Seth Godin, Sir John Hegarty, Gay Hendricks, Sally Hogshead, Russell Hyde, Susan Jeffers, Dean Jorgensen, Heather Lloyd-Martin, Dr Robert Lustig, Mark Manson, Roddie McVake, Michaela Merten, Lucia Montanarella, Nick Moore, Anna Moras-Spencer, Charlotte Mouncey, Luke Norman, Neil Oughton, Professor Steve Peters, Steven Pressfield, Simon Preston, Zahra Priddle, Paul Radford, Jon Robinson, Sir Ken Robinson, Hilda Rodriguez, Indy Samrai, Sheryl Sandberg, Suraj Sodha, Dave Talbot, Graham Taylor, Sam Taylor, Brian Tracy, Carl Uminski, Gary Vaynerchuk.

INTRODUCTION

Come on, let's get serious for a minute: have you read *Pazzabaijan* yet?

No?! What do you mean 'no'?! What do you mean, 'What is it?'!

Ok, no problem. I'll get over it.

Well, in case you *don't* know, *Pazzabaijan* was my first book. It was quite short, like this one. I like short books because I'm much more likely to finish them. I wasn't a big reader as a boy because books seemed so loooong (and a bit boring, but don't tell anyone I said that).

And now you're reading this one. Brilliant. Thank you.

What's it about? And why have I written it?

Well, it's about something which is quite important, in my opinion: how we think.

Why have I written it? Because I think we think quite a lot as humans, but I don't think schools teach us how to think because they think – at least *someone* does – that we'll manage without somebody actually pointing out what we do and why we do it. Don't you think?

But why should we just 'manage'? What if we were all taught early in our lives that how we think is partly down to nature and partly down to our choices?

For example, you might think more clearly about numbers and maths problems than you do about words and language. Those, I think, are based on nature and how your brain naturally works.

But your behaviour and reactions to things going on around you in life, I think, are based on choices you make, whether you realise you're making those decisions or not.

Let's say, for example, your phone misbehaves and you lose all your WhatsApp messages. Every single message from every thread.

Yes, that can be really annoying and frustrating but how do you react to things like that when they happen to you? Do you get angry? Do you cry? Do you wonder why things like this always happen to you?

Or do you put it down to one single piece of bad luck or bad hardware that's not the end of the world?

I think we should know inside our heads, and that we're all vulnerable to not knowing the answers to things or understanding the reasons behind our actions, and that it's OK to not have a Scooby-Doo what's going on.

But it's far better when we do. Life tends to be a bit easier when we understand a situation and how to deal with it

I like thinking. I think it's important.

And I want to help young people like you because I was oblivious to all this stuff until recently.

I could've done with a little book like this when I was your age to help me make sense of what was going on inside my head and around me.

So in my 30s (I'm 45 now), I started reading and learning a few things. (I'd left school by then).

And I discovered that a few people far cleverer than I am were talking and writing about the same idea, and each person gave this idea their own name.

One clever man called Professor Steve Peters wrote a book which has become known in our house as *The Monkey Book*. Its real name is *The Chimp Paradox*. Another clever man, Seth Godin, often talks and writes about 'the 'lizard brain'. And a third, Steven Pressfield, calls it 'the resistance'. There are probably others who talk about the same thing.

So what is it? I'll tell you.

It's that feeling you have when you are trying to get somewhere or achieve something and you're doing great but then you walk smack bang into a mental barrier.

It might be a little voice in your head telling you that you are no good, or that what you are doing is pointless or too hard.

Or it might be a gut feeling that seems so strong that it could physically stop you in your tracks.

There is a reason for this little voice, and it's a good one.

A lot of the time, we don't think as human beings. A lot of the time, we think like an animal thinks in the jungle.

And all that animal wants to do is survive, eat and make little animals.

When that animal is faced with something new or something which is clearly a problem for it, it often does one of two things. It often either fights or takes flight.

In other words, the animal tackles the threat it feels or it runs away.

We have that way of thinking, and the human way of thinking, and they confuse us all and can sometimes even cause us to have arguments with the people around us.

As you get older, mental barriers can stop you from being creative or inventive because being creative and putting what we've made out into the public leaves us with a feeling of vulnerability.

We have no idea how the thing we've made is going to go down with people.

That little animal's voice inside our head wants us to stay safe. The older we get, the more it seems to want us to keep our creativity to ourselves so that other people don't laugh at us or think we're ridiculous or our boss doesn't fire us.

This is pretty normal and happens to everyone but if you train your brain to keep thinking things through, then you might just open yourself up to a world of discovery and learning.

In a society where we are taught to think and behave like everyone else, this kind of creative freedom can take a lot of courage, strength and insight. After I left school, I had to learn how to allow myself to be creative again.

There was the odd failure (I'll tell you the story of one of these later in the book) but that's OK because progress and discovery often come from failure.

Everybody has talent but to make the most of it, we need to be wrong from time to time.

As educational focus moves to preparing students for the demands of university and a career, creativity is pretty much ignored at school, especially high school. As another clever man, Sir Ken Robinson, said: "If you're not prepared to be wrong, you'll never come up with anything original."

Being original and creative is quite important.

Think of all the things you like. Your favourite song at the moment, that footballer's tricks you saw the other day, even your phone. They all started out as someone's creative idea that needed practice and development.

In this book, I give that little animal's voice a name. I call it Mr Lizard.

DO ANYTHING YOU WANT TO

There is this Mr Lizard
And he never goes away
He's always there beside you
Regardless of the day

He's a funny little thing
He's your friend and then he's not
You've got to keep your eye on him
Or he'll just run amok!

Yes, you can do anything you want to if you make good choices.

Be aware that there's this character. He's pretty impulsive, doesn't always make the right choices, and can be a bit rash.

He lives somewhere very close to you and he's called Mr Lizard.

In fact, he lives inside you. He's inside your head.

And the amazing thing is, we *all* have our own Mr Lizard inside our head. And he's a very confusing little so-and-so.

Mr Lizard lives by different rules to us, you see.

Lizard can be a half-friendly, lovable, cuddly creature, who's on your side.

And he can be a half-confusing, irrational, naughty thing who *says* he's always on your side but you really don't know whether he truly means it.

So, we have two real problems here:

The first is that Mr Lizard can sometimes be really helpful, like he's our best friend, while at other times he can be our worst enemy.

The second problem is that because we think like animals first and humans second, we sometimes struggle to know when we're using animal instincts and when we're using thoughts based on who we are as humans, which come from our own background, experiences and how we're taught to behave by parents and teachers and brothers and sisters.

So, a lot of the time, we don't think as human beings. A lot of the time, we think like an animal thinks in the jungle.

The trouble is, it's normal. Mr Lizard isn't going anywhere. Ever. He is your best friend *and* your worst enemy.

Life is easier when you know how to deal with him. And I'll tell you how later in the book.

More on thinking. Think about this:

Conscious thinking is the thinking we do when we're actually thinking about it. Simple, right? ;-) Like deciding to hit the ball in rounders, or following a recipe when you're baking.

Unconscious thinking, on the other hand, is when ideas and questions come to us in the shower or during PE or when you're looking out of the window, daydreaming, during maths.

Mr Lizzy McLizardface is sometimes resistant to new people and situations and he gets bored. And when he's bored, he gets into trouble.

He needs feeding and needs to play regularly and frequently.

He can be funny, generous and really great company one minute but confusing, selfish and horrible the next.

He's got that whole 'best friend/worst enemy' thing going on. He sometimes says things off the cuff, without really thinking.

He might hate zip wires, and heights generally, and anything else that he thinks will hurt him, either physically or emotionally. He might be scared of water, or dogs, or jet skis. He almost certainly hates speaking in front of a big group of people.

And there are also things that he loves.

Sometimes, you can't trust him or rely on him, because he's wrong a lot of the time. But not all the time.

He's sometimes a commentator and sometimes he's your coach (more on that later).

How do you even handle someone like that?

Mr Lizard's thinking is five times more powerful than the human part of our brain, so we're always playing catch-up. Everyone is.

People who have come to know Mr Lizard and understand him tend to be the kind of people who are friendlier and more relaxed. These people are often better at what they do and might be able to respond to certain situations more effectively because they know what they are thinking and know why they are thinking it. They also know how to change or discard thinking that doesn't serve them.

You know the feelings you get when you do something that might be a little scary? Stuff like your first day at school, going on your first date, performing in a talent show or having to sit a particularly scary exam?

You might have felt nervous. Or you might have thought that everything's going to go horribly wrong and that people will laugh at you and you won't know where the toilet is and that when you ask someone they'll look at you as if you've just transported down from Mars and then you'll slip over on the floor in front of everyone and even more people will laugh at you and the teachers will think you're a numpty then the whole school will find out and you'll get bullied and it'll all just be one big horrible nightmare that'll haunt you forever.

So, you feel scared. You feel like you want to stay in your room and not go to your new school or on that first date or be in the talent show.

Sometimes, it feels far safer to just sit it out, to hide and go on Snapchat to do your streaks.

And that's Mr Lizard thinking for you. He's telling you to be careful and not put yourself in the way of harm. He just wants you to survive.

But really, deep down, you know that feeling worried is normal and necessary in order to survive and thrive in the long run.

A MESSAGE TO YOU RUDY

So, we think using different parts of our brain. Sometimes we think sensibly – like a real human being! That's when we're thinking consciously.

And sometimes we think more emotionally and without actually *thinking* much at all. That's when we're thinking unconsciously.

It's at these times that we 'go with our gut', we decide to do what we *feel* is right. It's that whole 'head versus heart' thing that you might have heard about.

Know which part Mr Lizard lives in? He's settled nicely in the unconscious part.

And remember that bit about Mr Lizard being both our best friend and our worst enemy? A lot of this book is about the latter.

For instance, when I started going bald (not that long ago, and I used to have hair halfway down my back), it was my own Mr Lizard who'd tell me that it was a bad thing: "Going a bit thin on top there, are we? Oh no!"

And one day, Mischa, my younger daughter, said: "Why don't you get a tattoo on your head of your hair, in memory of it?"

Very funny, yes (thank you Mischa!). And it played right into Mr Lizard's little green hands. Oh dear.

But what about him actually being *useful*? That's when he's our best friend.

You know those times when you get two offers of things to do on a Saturday, and you can't decide which to choose? And one of the things just feels more 'right' than the other? That's Mr Lizard and his amazing crystal ball trying to point you in the right direction.

And that time when you meet a friend of a friend for the first time. Something inside you that you can't quite put your finger on either pulls you towards that person like a giant magnet or pushes you away, as if to warn you about something you have no idea about but you just *feel it*.

That's Mr Lizard, too.

And he's also on hand when you're with friends (and maybe one or two people you don't know) and you're all in the park. Then someone pulls out a cigarette and you immediately think, 'Hang on, er, I'm not sure about this. Actually, I *am* sure. And this doesn't feel like the right thing for me, so I'm going to make up an excuse in a minute and go home or to the shop with those others who also said they wanted to go to the shop, and not smoke or be bullied into doing something I don't want to do.'

That's our lizardy friend, too.

Unconscious thinking is also how our brain operates when we're doing simple, mundane tasks that we've done loads of times before, like getting dressed.

Which is why my friend's mum once left her house wearing shoes from two different pairs (and one shoe was flat and the other had a high heel)!

She was tired and had put shoes on every day for years and years and put them on that particular time *without thinking.* You do this all day without even realising it.

Conscious thinking becomes unconscious thinking at times. An example of this comes soon after you learn to drive: one day, you realise that you've driven from A to B without having to concentrate so hard on gear changes and looking in the mirror and so on.

Before I learned to drive, a man came to our college and spoke to us about driving. What to expect, what it's like and similar stuff.

And I've always remembered one particular thing he said: he told us that, on average, drivers aren't concentrating for about one third of the time we spend behind the wheel. One third! Well, if we're not concentrating on driving, what are we thinking about? And how are we driving? Unconsciously, definitely; poorly, maybe.

And unconscious thinking is what guides us when we're unsure, which is why Mr Lizard's little den is in there, because that's what he specialises in.

So Mr Lizard can be correct. And he can be incorrect.

When you drive to the same destination, day in, day out, maybe for your job, you might get into your car one day with the intention of driving to the shops or to a friend's house but, before you know it, you're driving to work again.

You're following the route you take every working day unconsciously and out of habit.

The key thing to remember is that you have the choice to decide if Mr Lizard is correct or incorrect.

Another time when Mr Lizard is actually quite helpful is when you get that feeling that your friends are talking negatively about you, or making gestures and jokes that you don't follow or get just because they know (or at least *think* they know) that you won't get the joke.

In cases like this, it's worth listening to your little lizardy pal and asking yourself if those friends are actually friends.

And how do you do that? If only there was a quick, simple, easy method...

Ha! There is! And it's called the Motorway Service Station Test.

Imagine you're in the car, on the motorway. Then you need to make a stop, so you pull into the next service station and you get out of the car.

You walk towards the bit where the shops and toilets are and you spot someone you know.

It's one of these 'friends', but they haven't seen you.

And because they haven't seen you, it's totally up to you whether you go and say hello to that person.

If you don't, they won't even know about it. Ever. So they can't make you feel bad for not saying hello.

And if you do, you've simply seen a friend and said hello to them, as friends do.

The important bit is this: if you feel that you'd like to say hello, take time out of your journey and theirs, and will probably get a nice greeting back from that person, then they have passed the test. They are probably a true friend.

But if you feel that no, you don't want to go up to them, they look busy and rushed (that could be Mr Lizard's observation, by the way, rather than yours) or look like they're in a bit of a mood, and you decide not to go and say hello, they probably aren't a true friend, because if they were, it wouldn't matter how busy or upset they look. There's *always* time for a very quick hello from a friend.

So, are you fussed about them? Do you like them enough to say hello, even if you're both busy and clearly on your way somewhere with your families?

Or can you live without them, today and every day? Are they a bit rude?

Mr Lizard, *sometimes*, does send a message that helps.

And he's Chief Adjudicator of the Motorway Service Station Test.

LIFE'S WHAT YOU MAKE IT

Do you ever wonder what gown-up life is really like?

- Who gives you a job?

- What happens if you don't like the job?

- How do you pay taxes?

- How do you get your own home?

- How do you make new friends?

- How do you know what to do when you are at an airport, or move to a new school, or start a new job?

When I was a young lad, I had no clue about what grown-up life would involve. I thought I knew. Then, as soon as I stepped into a more grown-up world, I started to learn some pretty valuable lessons.

Like that time when I started studying in Leicester, and I used to go to a little café for a full English breakfast in the mornings before lectures.

I was too daft to realise that I was spending money in there that I couldn't afford to spend.

Then one day, the lady who worked in there asked me: "Are you a student?"

"Yeah," I replied, like Rodney Trotter (a bit of a gormless character from a popular English sitcom).

"Well how can you afford to keep eating in here then?" she said.

"Er..."

Her question was fair. I thought about my answer.

That was the last time I ever visited that café.

At £2.20 for a full English, which was a lot of money back then (well, it was about £2.20!) my regular visits were a bit daft. Why couldn't I make my own breakfast, or buy a cheaper one elsewhere?

The lady had raised my awareness of budgeting, which is a really important part of adult life. Living within your means is important so you don't get yourself into a financial hole when you're older.

I'd visited that café every day out of habit. A bit like the habit of driving the same route every day. I never thought about why I went to the café or how much it was costing me. Sometimes it takes other people to point out peculiarities in your own behaviour.

So, as you grow older, and begin to look after yourself more and rely on adults less, there's no limit to your adventure. Yes, there are sometimes tricky questions to answer and some pretty dangerous terrains to navigate. Challenges, for sure. But that's OK, that's good.

You'll be organised enough to handle an Arctic adventure. You'll easily adapt to this new world.

Do you have to do everything that feels awkward and/or uncomfortable? Absolutely not.

ENJOY YOURSELF

Why do you want to do your thing?

Everyone needs a reason why, a purpose.

Why does my friend Robbo organise a trip to Munich for himself and a load of mates every year?

Because he loves organising? Because he knows a weekend away needs direction and he's the best man for the job? Or because he knows no one else will do it if he doesn't?

You'd have to ask him.

Why does anyone do anything that matters?

It could be that you're in a job you don't enjoy, but it's only temporary and it means you can save some money to pay for a holiday with your friends.

It could be that you're happiest when you're playing football or painting or baking or learning Shotokan, and *that's* why you do it.

Or it could be that you want to go to music college and become a professional drummer, and deep down you know you have to dig in and do the work for your GCSEs so that you can actually get in to music college.

There are a million reasons why people do stuff, and the best ones are just because they want to or because they enjoy it.

My reason for doing stuff used to be to have as much fun as possible. When I got older and had children I realised that it was no longer just about me. There were other people who needed my time as well for fun and other stuff, like changing nappies. Smelly 'fun'.

But before then, I used to enjoy myself a bit too much.

In 1994, when I lived in Pinner and was working at HMV Trocadero, which was near Piccadilly Circus, I used to go out in London's West End all the time, having fun. And I used to fall asleep on the train home. All the time.

Funny, yeah, until you find you're spending all your money on cabs back from the end of the Metropolitan line when you've drifted off on the last train of the night again.

On my last day of work there, they gave me an England football top. It was a really nice one and I was delighted with it. They also gave me a t-shirt that said *Wake me up at Pinner* across the front, which made me laugh.

What's *your* reason?

If you have passion, if you really believe in what you should be doing, you'll succeed.

IT'S A LONG WAY TO THE TOP

That title's from an AC/DC song. When AC/DC started, they played in pubs and at universities everywhere.

They became really good.

After spending years travelling up and down motorways in an old van to play more shows and writing more songs, they got better and better at their work.

There's a famous idea that I read in a book called *Outliers* by Malcolm Gladwell that says to be really, really good at something, you have to put in 10,000 hours of practice.

Practice that goes on for years and years.

Mrs Doubtfire – er, I mean Robin Williams, the comedian who played Mrs Doubtfire in the eponymous film – put in years of work performing comedy routines to tiny audiences before he made it big.

The Beatles, the most successful and most influential band in history, went to Hamburg in Germany and played lots and lots and lots of gigs then came back to Liverpool in England where they were from and started playing at the Cavern Club.

And, as pretty much everybody on the planet now knows, it turned out they were really good. Lots of people who heard them play loved them, then the rest of the world heard them play and they loved them as well.

And people still love them.

When Bill Gates founded Microsoft he dreamed of a day when one of his computers would be on every office desk in the United States. He started as a simple programmer.

He put in 10,000 hours of practice, too.

When all his friends were out playing, he was indoors. On his own. Programming. Sad? I don't think so. He was getting really, really good at his thing.

If you have a dream of doing a certain thing and becoming really good at it and successful and getting well paid for it, you have to put in *a lot* of practice. That takes discipline (which I've heard defined as the difference between what you want and what you want now).

The temptation to give up when you've already put in loads of work but feel it's not getting you anywhere is normal, but remember this: people normally feel that way *just before* they're about to get a breakthrough that changes everything for them.

Almost nothing works the first time it's attempted. Just because what you're doing doesn't seem to be working, it doesn't mean it won't work. It just means that it might not work the way you're doing it.

Never stop investing in yourself. Never stop improving. Never stop doing something new.

Give yourself time.

There's an often-quoted line that says success is down to ten per cent inspiration and 90 per cent perspiration. What does that mean? It means you can have a great idea (inspiration) but without a lot of work (sweat/

perspiration) to bring your idea to fruition, absolutely nothing happens.

Your idea is like a wheelbarrow: it'll go nowhere without you pushing it.

You don't need a map for where you're going – good job, too, because there isn't one. You just need courage, experience and the ability to stick at it.

IT'LL BE EASIER IN THE MORNING

Most of the headings in this book are actually titles of some of my favourite songs.

But not this one.

I've never really listened to the song much, even though I bought the Hothouse Flowers album it's from when I was a teenager, but the title has always stayed with me.

I considered I Go To Sleep by The Kinks/The Pretenders/Sia, but that doesn't say what I want to say quite like the title I've chosen. Things are often easier in the morning, when you've had a good night's sleep.

Mr Lizard loves it when you're feeling tired. That's when he just *loves* to help out. Well, as usual, he *thinks* he's helping.

When you're tired, you don't do things as well as you can.

For example, you might not feel like making jokes even though you're able. But being able to laugh even when you're tired is *really* important.

Tiredness can make us feel less confident, which is when we can let things get on top of us more easily.

And that opens the door for you-know-who to pop his little head in:

"Hello!" says Mr Lizard. "Only me! Feeling a little bit wobbly in yourself? Don't worry, I'm used to working at times like this. You just leave things to me."

So with you yawning and leaving your mental door wide open, Mr Lizard's ready and willing to step in and 'help'.

When I was younger, long before I knew any of this stuff, I used to sit and listen to the conversation going on around me and realise that I had little to contribute. So I'd stay quiet. For ages. Then, when someone asked for my opinion or if I had a joke that was similar to the ones being shared by the group, I'd make an idiot of myself by saying very little and getting my words mixed up.

So that just made me want to stay quiet again, even though I was happy to be there.

Looking back, I reckon this was tiredness. My lack of energy led to a lack of participation which in turn led to a drop in confidence.

After rest, that kind of scenario, in my experience at least, is less likely to happen.

And that's important to understand.

Why?

Because confidence is *so* important. It's the key to life: with it, you can do anything; without it, you're stuck. It was a bit of a shame then that I didn't have a lot of it when I was younger.

When I was about ten, me and my classmates at school were putting on some kind of show to celebrate the place where I lived (Pinner) being really old or something. I and a few other kids had to learn this old English dancing called morris dancing.

I was so rubbish at it, the teachers couldn't trust me to be a dancer, so they gave me a horse's head on a stick (don't worry, it wasn't a real horse's head) and told me to stand at one end of the actual morris dancers. They told me it was an important role but I knew I'd been demoted and felt stupid, embarrassed and a bit of a let-down.

So I stood there with a horse's head on a stick watching as the other kids got all the applause and lapped up the glory of being a morris dancer.

And also, around the same age, I was a centre-forward in the Sunday football team I played for. Trouble was, I wasn't very good at being a centre-forward. I was fast, and had a decent kick, but I didn't score many goals.

And if you know anything about football, you probably know that a centre-forward's main job is to score goals.

In fact, I didn't score any goals.

None at all.

I became known among my mates as The Striker Who Never Scored because I was the only centre-forward in the league who didn't score during the whole season.

Anyway, confidence. It's important.

And getting good sleep helps.

When you're tired, you're less sure of yourself. You're more likely to make mistakes.

You might lose patience or get into an argument or, at times, say nothing at all when it'd be much better for you to speak up. Or maybe you just stay quiet and want to hide until the whole situation fades away.

When you're tired, Mr Lizard is on alert. He becomes a bit paranoid, watching out for comments or signs that he'll then dwell on just in case he needs to react to what he thinks is a threat. He sometimes sees bad in certain situations which are actually harmless.

He hears someone say something that he thinks is nasty or spiteful, but actually isn't. He might take something out of context and turn it into a big catastrophe that's really not bad at all.

Is Mr Lizard offering you ideas that are too sensitive or not based on reality?

Confidence comes from kip so get some rest.

BONUS TIP: want to know a great way to feel confident when you've got something important coming up?

Thought so.

You have two options (one choice).

You can either think how most people think, which is based on your belief that you can do something. So the more you reckon you'll be successful, the more confident you are.

Trouble is, that can lead to a lot of confidence or not much at all, which isn't helpful.

It's Mr Lizard's animal way of thinking. You can't guarantee that your ability will deliver the result you want, no matter how badly you want it.

So what's the alternative? What's the human way?

The human way is based on doing your best.

Tell Mr Lizard that you're going to do your best and that you'll handle the consequences no matter what they are.

You can always do your best. That, you *can* control.

WAKING UP

In 1995, I worked at another branch of HMV, this time in Brent Cross, in north London. In fact, it's where I met my wife, Shoelace.

Working there, I drove in every day and was late every day.

I'd race to get to the car park, anxious to make up a few seconds because I'd dithered at home before I left and wasted time.

In fact, I used to be late for everything. I was even late for my first date with Shoelace. That's not right. Making her wait in the rain outside the Hippodrome? What was I thinking? She ended up marrying me. Poor woman.

One day at HMV, I got to the car park and the attendant told me off, quite rightly, for driving too fast. It was dangerous.

I'd park my car and run up to the shop to start work. Fortunately, my boss liked me so never gave me a hard time over it. He always pointed out that I was late, but I carried on doing it.

Years later I was reading a book and it dawned on me that when you're late for things, you're actually being really selfish because you're disrespecting someone else's time as well as your own.

Being selfish is not something I've ever liked, so I quickly changed my ways. I realised that I couldn't blame it on traffic or trains or trying my best but still failing. There are always delays because of reasons you can't control, so don't add to them.

Waking up and getting up has never been easy for me. Do yourself a favour and allow plenty of time when you have to be somewhere at a certain time.

Go to bed early, get some proper sleep, and get up with time to spare so you don't have to rush or put people in danger because you're rushing or feel under pressure because you're late.

It's horrible when you're stuck on a train or in traffic and you're late for something important and there's nothing you can do to improve the situation. That opportunity came earlier.

Respect your own time and other people's. It's the one thing in life that's truly irreplaceable.

MIRROR IN THE BATHROOM

Before the internet, everyone read newspapers.

Kids would get a job at a paper shop (it's a wonder why they didn't blow away! Ha ha, sorry, terrible dad joke) delivering newspapers in the morning before school to all the houses down a road or two.

Papers were (and still are) either 'broadsheets' (because the sheets of paper they're printed on are broad, such as *The Times*, *The Daily Telegraph* and *The Guardian* in the UK) or tabloids (aka 'red tops'), like *The Sun*, *The Daily Star* and *The Daily Mirror*.

Broadsheets and tabloids are written in very different styles and people would read them while eating breakfast, sitting in the bath, sitting on the bus, during their lunch break at work, in the pub after work, on the way to football on a Saturday. Everywhere.

Everywhere you take your phone, in fact.

They'd read the *Mirror* in the bathroom.

Back then, just like today, the news was generally negative and bad because that's what sells.

On social media, however, the situation's different. People often post only the best bits of their lives.

They kind of airbrush the rubbish out of the picture – the difficult bits that they don't want anyone to see or know about. The troublesome bits, the boring bits, the mundane. Basically, all the *normal* stuff. They wipe those bits out of the picture completely. Some people are on a mission to highlight the bad bits, which is even worse.

The trouble is, everything looks perfect at a distance, and if you spend all your time looking at the best bits of other people's lives, you end up believing that you're the only one with a less-than-perfect situation.

And that focuses your attention on the differences between you and them, which isn't helpful at all.

That's where cybercondria comes from: health anxiety that people try to fix by going online and picking a condition with a scientific name that sounds about right.

Is that how doctors work? Of course not.

Use your phone to make a call and book an appointment if you have to, not to Google a random set of symptoms and self-diagnose what you haven't got.

Instead of comparing yourself to others, start thinking: 'Actually, what I have is pretty good.' Pretty, pretty, pretty good.

You might even, actually, you know, be *happy*. People get happiness and pleasure mixed up and confused all the time, which is a shame because they're two of our most important and positive emotions. Lots of people think happiness and pleasure are exactly the same, but they're not.

Pleasure is short-lived, happiness is long-lived. Pleasure – when you think *'This feels good, and I want more'* – is about taking rather than giving, it can be achieved with substances or computer games or food and is often experienced alone.

Happiness, on the other hand, is when you think *'This feels good, and I don't want or need any more'*. It's about giving, can't be achieved with substances and is usually experienced with other people.

Amazing things happen inside our head when we're feeling happy or experiencing pleasure.

Pleasure releases a chemical inside our brain called dopamine and happiness releases a chemical called serotonin.

Dopamine and serotonin help our brain cells (neurons) talk to each other.

When neurons talk to each other and dopamine is present, they get excited and tell their friends.

But when they get too excited, too often, they die, so the neurons turn off their bits that get excited so that they don't all die.

That's why some people try to get a buzz by maybe doing a higher bungee jump or going on a bigger rollercoaster. They need to get more of their neurons excited than the last time because some of them have died out.

In the end, you could go on the biggest rollercoaster of them all but feel no pleasure as a result.

But when serotonin is involved, neurons slow down, they don't get too excited and they don't tell their friends.

That's happiness.

But the thing is, the more pleasure we try to get, the less happy we feel.

And the media, from *The Sun* to Snapchat, confuse happiness and pleasure. And that confuses us.

It's why adverts try to get us to buy things – so that we think we can buy happiness when actually they want us to buy pleasure.

Trouble is, more people are unhappy these days than ever before. Everything that makes us happy are the things that we can't buy. Sounds corny but it's true.

Which is why looking at Snapchat, Instagram and Facebook for hours every day doesn't do you any good.

Every time you get a notification on your phone, the dopamine gets excited neurons talking to their friends, and makes you look at your phone more often and stay on it for longer.

Some people think that if they show themselves on social media as they really are, everyone will abandon them.

That's not true.

What is true is that people who spend most of their time on Facebook, Snapchat and Instagram, but don't see their friends in person very often, are the most likely to feel lonely, left out of things and wish they had more good friends. (Mr Lizard: "I'm nervous about what people think and are going to say. It sometimes bugs me when I don't get a certain amount of likes on a picture.")

Mobile phones have exposed more and deeper vulnerabilities and can actually lead to depression.

Recognise what you're good at and be grateful for what you have.

It's much better to be yourself and appreciate who you are and what you have than compare yourself to anyone else.

JUST DANCE

"It always feels better when you're able to be yourself, to just be you. And being you means not being afraid or ashamed of sharing the gift that you've been given."

Stevie Wonder

I used to have very long hair but now I use clippers on almost the shortest setting. I guess my hair went on holiday and never came back.

But before all that, a long time ago, there was one occasion – the *only* occasion – when I did something different with my hair.

I was 13 and getting ready to go to my first concert: Howard Jones at Wembley Arena, with my mate Big Al. It was 1985.

Howard Jones had this blond, spiky hair-do, typical eighties style. I had dark hair that was too long and too fine to do anything similar with.

But it didn't stop me trying.

Big Al must've thought I looked ridiculous when he came to my house so we could get the bus to the station, and my hair had this lump pushed up in the middle like I'd slept under the bed with my head squashed up against a suitcase. Still, Big Al's very polite and I don't remember him sniggering.

What was I thinking? I think I was trying to be creative and express myself, but without the practice or experience to do it well. But you might find that practising to express yourself is worth the effort and persevering with.

What *does* it take to be creative? Having valuable ideas takes a desire to make or produce something rather than just consume all day. It could be music, a cake, a story, a video, anything.

Consuming means playing games, reading what your friends are doing on Snapchat and Instagram, watching Netflix and things like that.

Maybe don't get an iPad, get a notebook – a real one, with paper and everything.

If you're going to consume, absorb knowledge that will help you.

Sir John Hegarty has worked in television advertising in Britain for ages. He says that to be creative takes fearlessness.

So even in my blind, hopeless devotion to Howard Jones, I suppose I was acting fearlessly. I was just doing my hair how I wanted and didn't care what people thought.

Creativity is doing what you feel, rather than what you think other people will like.

Where do ideas actually come from?

Mr Hegarty said – and I agree – that if you consume rubbish (food, music, information that's wrong or unhelpful or both, jokes, and everything else), you'll produce rubbish.

I also believe that whatever is within us has to come out. It always does. It's like water: it finds a way to leak through.

That includes stuff we put into our minds and bodies (food, music, social media posts – everything) and stuff that we've experienced and inherited (including how we handle certain situations).

Lady Gaga, whose real name is Stefani Joanne Angelina Germanotta and who's got millions of followers online and hundreds of millions of dollars in the bank, is very normal in other respects. She's human. Just like Taylor Swift, Katy Perry, Bieber, Jess Glynne and Paul McCartney are human beings. They just happen to be very famous human beings.

But there's a difference with Lady Gaga: she gets depressed.

She cries in agony and searches for answers when she's with her doctor, as her painful condition wears her down.

She's vulnerable, just like you and me and everyone else. If anything, she's *more* vulnerable. She suffers with pain, sleep deprivation, relationship heartbreak and loneliness.

Emotional and physical pain are real, and pretending they're not leads to suffering. The trouble is, pain doesn't show up on a body scan and can't be measured in a test. Pain always catches up with us, so we shouldn't deny it exists.

One reason I like Gaga is because she tries to get rid of the negativity that lots of people feel when they admit to having physical and/or emotional pain. She doesn't try to hide the actual pain.

Some people use their pain as a kind of crutch, a companion, even their best friend.

Some people deal with emotional pain by fighting, drinking, gambling or taking drugs. They use them to block out what they're feeling inside, whether they know that that is what they are doing or not.

Other people use their pain much more positively. They're productive with it. They paint pictures, write, cook or bake because of it, or express themselves on a football pitch or with a guitar or a pair of drum sticks. Or they design graphics and get hired by a really famous company to create a logo and come up with something imaginative and relevant.

For example, have you spotted the white arrow in the middle of the FedEx logo? I like that design because it's a very creative use of a symbol we all recognise.

The white arrow in the middle of the logo is relevant to FedEx because it suggests movement, which FedEx provides for packages and parcels. The company moves packages and parcels around the world for people and businesses. The whole planet sees the arrow but not everyone notices it.

So find a fun and productive way to express yourself. You are good at something – *really* good. Use it, it's a strength. Whether you feel any pain or not (and lucky you if you don't – you're in the minority), find a positive way to express what's inside because it *will* come out. You might as well be in charge of it.

Emotional pain is why Gaga has an album called *Joanne* – she's still upset over the death of her aunt Joanne, who died in 1974, which was years before Gaga was even born.

Mexican painter Frida Kahlo is also really famous. She made art after she was seriously injured and nearly died in a road accident which caused her pain and medical problems for the rest of her life. She'd dreamt of becoming a doctor but then, because she could no longer pursue this dream, it inspired her creativity.

There are loads of songs about the pain of having no money, or feeling rejected and heartbroken, inspired because the people who created them all suffered some sort of pain.

So if you feel pain, you might find it useful to express how you're feeling. Draw, dance, write, pick up a guitar or work in a garden or do whatever it is that you like to do.

One thing to bear in mind though is that the first version of anything is usually rubbish, no matter who you are or what experience you have. Version 1 is not going to be as good as Version 2.

I wrote a book once called *Naughty By Nature*. It took me two years to finish the first version. I didn't do much work to sell the book after writing it and it just sat on my computer for a few years.

Then one day, I had an idea to put the whole thing out on Twitter, line by line. Eighty-one thousand words.

Towards the end of doing that, I prepared to sell the book again. I hired someone to design the cover, and had another person lined up to format my work so that I could sell it as an ebook, and I eventually took up the offer of my good friend Susan, who'd asked if I wanted her to edit the book.

Suze did such a great job but, in the end, I didn't go through with self-publishing *Naughty By Nature.*

I'd finished the first version but it wasn't very good. I didn't realise this myself though. Suze pointed it out to me (very respectfully, I must add!). My book had never gone further than a first draft because I was too lazy to improve it, and it showed.

You might want to produce something just for you, in private, and that's fine. But you might want to put your thing out into the world, which is also great. But remember: Version 1 of anything is usually rubbish so you might want to improve it.

Work hard and follow your heart. Just dance and use what you have. Use the hand you're dealt, as someone once told me.

Use your creativity because it's like no one else's.

When you're creating something and expressing yourself, you might find that you forget about time and that what you're doing feels very natural, like you hardly have to think about it.

But later, when the time comes to put your creation out into the world, if that's what you've decided to do, that's a different story. It's normal to feel doubt and fear, and wonder what on earth you're thinking. The trick here is to carry on. If you've decided to make your work public, be brave and ignore the little voice in your head that tells you to keep your creation to yourself and out of harm's way.

Thank Mr Lizard for his suggestion, but decline following up on it.

REBEL REBEL

If you take nothing else from this book, take this bit.

There are certain things to remember that can make your life so much easier and calmer.

Our problem is that Mr Lizard gets in there first. We think like animals before we think like humans. All the time. Mr Lizard is five times more powerful.

So when something happens that annoys or upsets you, remember that there are certain truths in life for all of us:

1. Life is not fair (so make your own breaks). Take responsibility and don't blame

2. The goalposts move (parents, friends, teachers and bosses change their minds; and rules can change, sometimes without anyone telling you)

3. There are no guarantees (meaning some things won't turn out how you want or expect them to)

Rebel against what you don't like but do yourself a favour and remember those things.

And when you start driving, there's another one to add to the list:

4. Lots of people drive without respect, courtesy or patience. Don't be one of them

When we lived in central Watford, our road and all the surrounding roads were packed with Victorian terraced houses, so they were quite narrow streets and there were always loads of cars parked down each side.

Occasionally, there'd be a gap, which was handy to park in and also handy for people to let other drivers pass because the roads were only wide enough for one car to go up or down.

I was driving near our house one day when I saw a car near the bottom of the road, so I waited in the only gap I could see. I was near the top of the road. I thought it'd just be easier if I stopped and waited because I couldn't see the situation at the other end and couldn't be sure if that driver was going to stop even if he could.

So I'm sitting there, waiting for this car to come up towards me and pass, which it did. But as it approached me, my own Mr Lizard reminded me very quickly that this person should thank me for my kindness.

Stupidly, I followed Mr Lizard's suggestion and tried to persuade the other driver to thank me by thanking him with a friendly hand gesture of my own (that was fuelled by anger).

The driver got closer. And Mr Lizard got angrier: "He's not going to thank me! He's not thanking me! Rude git!"

Of course I followed Mr Lizard's suggestion that this person wasn't grateful, and I quickly switched my friendly hand gesture to a much less friendly one, and I put on my best 'angry' face, too.

The other driver saw this switch and, straight after passing my car, drove around the mini roundabout that was just behind where I'd been waiting and came up behind me all aggressively and followed me!

Oh no! Mr Lizard had very quickly led me into trouble! All this happened within ten seconds (our Mr Lizards work fast because they want to protect us and, in the jungle, there's no time to waste, no mucking about, when something much bigger or quicker than you wants to eat you!).

I drove faster than I should've down the road next to ours, desperately trying to lose this lunatic behind me who I'd sworn at just because he didn't say thank you.

Is that really a good reason to get into a fight? Is there *any* good reason to get into a fight, if you're not a boxer?

Someone told me once: "Never poo on your own doorstep." I wish Mr Lizard had been listening at the time.

I couldn't go straight home because the lunatic (he almost certainly wasn't a lunatic, just a normal bloke who didn't like being sworn at – when he might have thanked me anyway) was following me at speed. So I ended up driving around until I lost him so I could go home safely.

Whether or not that man was going to thank me for waiting for him, lots of drivers are courteous and thank you for waiting for them or letting them out of the side road into the main road you're driving on. But there are lots who don't. And there's nothing you, I or anyone else can do about it.

I can't let them wind me up.

I have to feed Mr Lizard the banana that tells him to ignore rude, disrespectful drivers. Don't try to change them one by one with a V sign. They probably won't like it and will chase you down the road.

And the same goes for those other three truths: things happen in life that aren't fair, and there's nothing you can do about it.

Imagine a football match where one team has got the ball and scores a really good goal, then the referee blows her whistle and says, "No goal, the goalposts are over there now and you just missed."

Sometimes, things change at the last minute, or that girl you don't get on with gets invited to the sleepover that you were really looking forward to, or the talent show song you were practising hard gets changed.

It happens. And you have to accept it. It's nobody's fault. These things happen to everyone all the time. Don't complain about it or swear at people.

When you remember these things, it's much harder for life to upset you.

RATHER BE

What else does Mr Lizard like, apart from bananas? He likes what he knows, what he understands and what he's sure is safe.

So that means he doesn't like the unknown, because – to him, at least – he doesn't understand it and it's not safe.

Are you an athlete? Even if you're not, imagine you are, and that you've made it through to the final of the 100 metres in a competition for all the kids in your area. Parents will be there to watch, even the local newspaper will be, too. It's the first time you've raced at this high level.

You walk with the other runners towards the track to take your place on the start line. And then, when you least expect or want him to, Mr Lizard pops up, expressing – very clearly and with a very worried urgency – that what you're doing is wrong and silly. It's not, according to him, very brave. It's stupid.

"Come on," he says. "Think about this. You don't want to look silly in front of all these people when you finish in last place. Imagine it! No, let's sort something out so that you stay safe, in familiar territory."

The starter says, in a loud voice, "Take your marks," and the people in the crowd fall silent. The tension mounts, and expectation is in the air.

Mr Lizard stands in the back of your mind, watching with his arms folded. He is not smiling.

"Set...," says the starter, and...

Bang!

The starting gun goes off and you and the other athletes rise out of your blocks and race away down the track.

You're doing well! You're in second place!

Mr Lizard winks at you, lights a cigar, and folds his arms again as he puffs away like a chimney, as you consider how you're going to respond.

Then, ouch! Your leg! The left one! It really hurts!

You pull up, and watch in pain as the sprinter who'd been leading the race drops to third, overtaken just before the line by two others.

Where did they come from?! And what happened to your leg?

Mr Lizard drops his cigar and stubs it out on the floor with a bright green foot.

His work is done – and so is your hamstring.

What happened there? You could've won but you didn't.

Now, maybe you didn't win because you didn't warm up properly or you might have overstretched.

Or maybe you didn't win because, deep down, you were scared of the changes in your life that winning would bring. Maybe winning would move you beyond your comfort zones, which can be a bit daunting.

Was the situation caused by a physical situation or a mental one? Maybe you didn't warm up properly because you weren't relaxed and following your normal pre-race routine.

What if it was Mr Lizard who stopped you from going to the Great Unknown?

Victory at a level you've never taken part in before, and all that goes with it: the next level of competition, with better athletes, more pressure to perform, more pressure to live and act like the fantastic athlete that you are.

So you and Mr Lizard stay safe, out of harm's way, in the village of Known, Familiarshire. Where nobody wins at anything or achieves anything or does anything remarkable.

It's a place where 60 per cent of lottery winners go back to having little or no money within two years of their windfall, having lost/given away/squandered/wasted their new wealth.

Suddenly having loads of cash is a scary thing for Mr Lizard because it's new and comes with responsibility, which he's not great with.

People often play it safe. They blend in and try not to be noticed. Those things are fine at first. For example, when you start at a new school or job, it's fine and normal to want to blend in during the early days, and assess the situation.

You look around and notice things. You pay attention to the new rules you need to learn. You watch to see who does what, why and when. What things are particular to that place that you haven't witnessed or experienced before, such as the language people use, the length of lunch break you get and the intensity of the work you're asked to do?

After the initial period, when you've been in the new place for a week or two, it's natural for you to feel more settled and comfortable.

After a while, blending in and trying not to be noticed is risky and dangerous.

Mr Lizard wants us to blend in because in the jungle that meant it was easier to stay alive. If you're not seen by a big, nasty animal with big, nasty teeth, it's less likely to eat you.

Mr Lizard, and Lizardry in general, are all about survival. Hence camouflage. Hence chameleons changing their skin to match their environment. Think Randall in *Monsters, Inc.*

Unfortunately, blending in, and being unremarkable – in other words, playing it safe – used to work but not any more.

You have to get out and stay out of your comfort zones because not much of any significance happens when you're in them.

Playing it safe is actually risky because blending in, when you're in the world of work, usually leads to other people being chosen for promotions and other freelancers being picked to do great work.

And only the most interesting, remarkable and different ideas are able to cut through all the noise.

In my own business, if I produce similar work to lots of other people, and sell it in the same way that everyone else sells themselves and their work, how am I going to be noticed by the people who I want to attract and be seen by?

By being different in a positive way so that I am noticed, not ignored.

When the good thing you're getting involved in, such as a big race at an important athletics meeting, is a bit scary because it's outside your comfort zones and in the Great Unknown, it makes you grow as a person and moves you closer to achieving your ambition.

In the Great Unknown, lottery winners seek help and advice from those who know better. They force their Mr Lizards to adjust and get used to the new surroundings.

Lizardry, in the Great Unknown, is managed. Carefully and attentively.

Where would you rather be?

AIN'T NO MOUNTAIN HIGH ENOUGH

When Mischa was about to leave junior school, she and the rest of her year-group put on the best school play I've ever seen. It was a brilliantly imaginative way of teaching kids about some of the new experiences they could expect following their transition to high school.

When I watched it with Shoelace, we realised why we'd heard Mischa singing *Ain't No Mountain High Enough* at home for a few weeks leading up to the performance.

I love a bit of Motown (it's what me and my mates used to listen to every weekend when we were sixteen) and this song fits perfectly around the idea of this chapter: values.

You have values, whether you realise it or not, and whether or not you've worked out what they are.

Are friends important to you? How do you treat other people? How do you get your work done? Do you try your hardest every time or do you cut corners and try to get away with doing as little as possible? Are you the sort of person who perseveres with things, even when it's tricky or easier to just give up?

What's important to you? How do you rate being generous? Are you loyal? Are you honest? Are you tolerant of people from other parts of the world? Do you put safety first? Do you look out for your friends, old and new?

Is family or work more important?

Those things are your values, and we all have them, and every business has them as well.

Here are two examples:

- It's nice to be important but it's more important to be nice

- Never say something behind someone's back that you wouldn't be prepared to say to their face

Metrics are how you choose to measure the things that are important to you, or how a company chooses to measure the things that are important to it, such as the number of visitors to their website, or the profit they made as a percentage of the revenue they earned.

How are you choosing to measure yourself? What really matters to you? Is it the number of friends you have? Be careful. It's better to have one real friend than ten people who'd ditch you just when you needed them. If you want to read more on the number of stable friendships we can actually sustain, Google 'Dunbar's number'.

How you choose to measure yourself when comparing your current position with where you want to be is important.

Jim Rohn, an American entrepreneur, author and motivational speaker who lived between 1930 and 2009, famously suggested that we are the average of the five people we spend the most time with.

Look at your family and the friends you spend most time with, either in person, on the phone, via Skype, FaceTime or smoke signals. Spend a minute or two thinking about the influence they have on you, what you get from them and what you give them.

How do your conversations turn out? Do you usually end up laughing? Are your chats negative or positive?

How do you/they feel when you say goodbye to each other?

You might find that you're most influenced by people or a person you don't actually know personally.

How?

Well they might be a musician and lyricist whose words and music you love listening to.

They could be the author of a non-fiction book or two that you enjoy reading.

They might have produced other work that's inspired you and influenced your own creativity.

Whatever the case for you, choose carefully.

I love having friends who each give me something different. With certain friends I talk mainly about football. With others, it's business and personal progress. Other friends are into music, like me, so we naturally talk about that a lot, while others inspire me through their creative endeavours.

All of these people do have two crucial things in common:

- They all have a good sense of humour
- They're all positive

Furthermore, I am incredibly lucky to have a brilliant, funny and positive family, too, who are always looking for the laugh in things and fun to be around.

That Jim Rohn chap that I mentioned above wrote a book called *Five Major Pieces to the Life Puzzle* in which he described what he felt were the five components of success:

- Philosophy – how you think
- Attitude – how you feel
- Action – what you do
- Results – measure often to see if you are making progress
- Lifestyle – the kind of life you can make for yourself out of the first four pieces

Having good people in your life who inspire you and push you towards better things is essential.

Who do you listen to? Is their influence good, bad or indifferent?

If you come across a time when a friend does something or says something that doesn't sit well with you, maybe that's a sign that their values don't match yours.

Maybe it's time to spend more time with people whose values you admire and share.

GETTING BETTER

I once worked on a client's book that featured a series of affirmations.

Affirmations are like telling Mr Lizard how it is, truths about yourself. And the best thing is this: you get to choose them.

When you have a set of affirmations, you're telling Mr Lizard to buzz off. Actually, what you're doing is telling *yourself* exactly how it is.

When you accept those affirmations as the truth, Mr Lizard has them on speed dial. You don't have to get involved.

How do you do that?

First, you need a set of affirmations that match your hopes, dreams, ambitions and values. To work effectively, affirmations must follow these four rules:

They must be:

1. In the present tense

2. In the first person

3. Positive, and contain no negative words

4. In the active voice

Write them down because using your hand and your brain at the same time helps you remember.

Next, you have to keep reading them, saying them to yourself, repeating them over and over until you think them automatically whenever you find yourself in a sticky situation (when Mr Lizard is trying to tell you something you don't want or need to hear).

Here are some affirmations that might be useful:

- I deserve the nice things that happen to me
- I am funny
- I am clever
- I am loved
- I handle pressures
- I am responsible and reliable
- I always try my hardest
- I learn from my mistakes
- I am organised
- I am a good listener
- I pay attention

SHAKE IT OFF

Like a lot of people, I used to think in terms of what wasn't there, what I didn't have and how I had to make do.

But I've never focused on bad luck.

Like the time when I was at football one Saturday, standing on a terrace, watching Watford. I was with my mates Sam and Big Al, and thousands of other people.

The terrace had no roof and behind us was a wall that separated it from Vicarage Road.

So, thousands of blokes, all standing there, packed in, no roof. Then someone on the pavement on the other side of the wall lobs a half-eaten hamburger over it. Guess whose head it landed on.

I could've focused on my bad luck.

But that's wrong because things like this happen to people all the time.

There's nothing you or I can do about it so focusing on bad things, inconveniences and negative situations puts them at the centre of our thinking, which makes laughing at the smaller, less serious moments of bad luck, like a half-eaten hamburger landing on your head, more difficult.

It's true what they say about laughter being the best medicine, so I find that by laughing at my own misfortune I forget that it can also be a bit of a pain.

Problems are unavoidable but you can choose *better* problems.

As Alan Titchmarsh, a really famous gardener, once said: "Nature's always generous." Look at leaves on the trees and pebbles on a beach. There's plenty! Plenty of everything.

But before you can take advantage of all the good stuff that's around, you have to bin the rubbish in your life.

Get rid of the clutter, the stuff that needs shaking off, whether it's a thought or even a way of thinking.

As you know, Mr Lizard talks to you in your head.

He can be either a commentator or a coach.

When he talks to you like a commentator, he says things like: "Ooh, that wasn't very good, was it?" and "Oh, she's not really ready for this yet." (HINT: no one's really ready for anything. You just have to think of Nike's slogan).

But when he's your coach, things are much happier: "Come on," he says, "you can do this!" Or "You can handle this situation because you've already shown that you can handle bigger situations that were worse than this one."

Ditch the negative 'commentator'.

Some things to think of – if something's not right or good enough, bin it. Shake it off:

- People in your life who aren't facing the same way as you (forwards, with a smile)

- Your job

- A pile of old bricks in your garden. I had such a pile, for months, after some kids kicked down my wall. It felt so good after I finally hired a skip and got rid of them (the bricks, not the kids)

- Decisions based on scarcity, lack, paranoia, insecurity or any other Mr Lizard-fuelled negative emotion

- A box full of stuff you haven't looked at in years

- Anything else that's redundant, useless, damaging, wasteful, greedy, boring or unreliable

Unfortunately, no matter what good things you do you'd still get the odd person (and they are odd) who'd find fault.

Best thing to do? Bin them – and their comment – and move on.

GOOD THING GOING

Finding a balance between keeping Mr Lizard happy and working out what you're good at can help you live a nice life.

Never let anybody push you around, whether they're in your head or the real world. You have just as much right to do what you're doing as anyone else, as long as it doesn't harm you or anyone else.

Make sure you read. Broaden your knowledge and interests by reading everything you can as often as you can. "You will be, in five years, who you are today except for the books you read and the people you meet." – Charlie 'Tremendous' Jones

Pay attention to your:

- Strengths
- Thoughts
- Home
- Feelings
- Hopes
- Dreams
- Achievements
- Failures
- Ideas

- Family and friends

- Clients/customers

- Habits

- Health

- Relationships

- Values

- Behaviour

Also pay attention to your responsibilities. That means tidying up after yourself, looking after the money you get for your birthday and doing your fair share of clearing up after the cat/dog/iguana. And it's getting your school uniform ready on a Sunday evening rather than when you're rushing around on a Monday morning.

Be aware of what you can control and change, and what you can't. If you don't like something that's within your control to change, such as your reaction to things, either change it or stop complaining, and choose something else to care about.

If you can't control something that's bothering you, then you have to accept it and move on.

As I said earlier: problems are unavoidable but you can choose *better* problems.

Mr Lizard will always be there so you'll never be free of him.

But you can put him in a place where he can serve you better and not fill you head with doubts and feelings that you don't want.

Then he'll love you and be very happy, and spend much more of his time being your best friend and much less being your worst enemy.

It's time to go from following rules to making them!

CONCLUSION

Everyone has their own Mr Lizard inside their heads so this is perhaps why you shouldn't take things that people say or do personally.

For example, if someone you know well behaves in an unusual way, you can perhaps understand it when you're aware of how they might be feeling, and why. Put yourself in their shoes.

Maybe they're anxious or nervous because of what's about to happen (such as an important meeting, performing on stage or an essential visit to the dentist to have a tooth taken out).

Or maybe they're in the presence of someone they really like or fear or who has some kind of power or influence over them.

All those things might make you think and behave differently.

Maybe one of the problems with learning how to think is that other people don't always understand how their own head works and people say and do stupid things as a result. It's their problem, not yours.

So I think you should think about thinking. Watch how you react when good things happen to you. Notice how you behave when something unpleasant happens to you. Pay attention to your life:

- The games you play,

- The things you say,

- The world that's all around you.

- The profiles, the pages,

- Their stories, their rages – keep friends around who ground you.

The main thing to remember is that thinking is not as simple as we think. Confusing and conflicting thoughts are normal.

Different periods in life affect your mental state differently.

But overall, life is better when you're able to step back from the emotions of a situation, do your best to gather your thoughts and find a point of focus to start sifting through the problem.

If you're feeling low or scared or worried or anxious or anything else negative, ask yourself if you want to feel that way.

If the answer's no, ask Mr Lizard exactly what he's worried about. Then let him answer you.

Mr Lizard will back down before you know it.

ABOUT THE AUTHOR

Paul Parry is a writer, blogger, editor and sub-editor who often works at major international sporting events such as the Olympic Games. He has worked on ten books, built dozens of websites and served as a magazine columnist.

Paul is also the father of two girls, Shiana and Mischa. He has been married to Sholée (Shoelace) since 2001 and Watford FC since 1982.

Having worked for twenty years in shops, warehouses and TV transmission suites, Paul took voluntary redundancy in 2013 to follow his passion for writing.

He is a partner in Amp Media, an editorial agency serving major international sports organisations, and lives with his family in Hertfordshire, England.

For news of future books and more information, go to paulparry.com/MrLizard.

You've finished! Enjoy your day.

Want to hear the songs whose titles make up this book?
A Spotify playlist is available – head to
paulparry.com/MrLizard